HUMAN RESOURCES

NOT

HUMAN REMAINS

PUSHING THE BOUNDARIES OF TRANSPARENCY TO THE POINT YOU COULD NOT MAKE THIS STUFF UP

TRACEY CHRYSTAL

Author: Tracey Chrystal

Title: Human Resources Not Human Remains

ISBN: 978-1-0686737-5-7

Category: Human Resources /Personnel Management / Business

This book is dedicated to every HR Person who turned up on Day 1 and was left to sweep up past mistakes! Before being able to sparkle and shine like the true talented STAR that you are!

Sometimes the right path is not the easiest one!

SMILE AND SPARKLE .... EVERYDAY

Human Resources not Human Remains

CONTENTS

Human Resources

[Hr-]

Noun
The unofficial lawyer, psychologist, event planner, teacher, peace maker, career planner, detective.

Prologue

I have established an HR Consultancy & Coaching business on the back of a dynamic professional career. An expert in the field of Human Resources and seen as a thought and influencing leader. Working with some of the largest companies on the globe, my international assignments have taken me to India, USA, Europe and widely across the UK. With extensive HR Experience of over 30 years plus, there have been highs and lows on my journey however, my legacy will be that I continue to grow with integrity and stay true to my authentic self.

Looking over the past decades I have held senior positions with DHL, Rolls Royce, PRA, University of Glasgow, Maritime Engineering, Rail, and IT.

One of my highs was the Head of HR role at Scottish Enterprise where the newly appointed First Minister presented me and my team with the Chairmans Award for winning the "SE The Apprentice/You're Hired."

In any Senior HR professional career there are of course lows and most of these come with the onset of change. While working for one of the most innovative and creative maritime engineering companies in 2020 I made a pivotal change and relaunched Chrystal HR & Coaching.

So, what does Chrystal HR & Coaching provide? The list is not exhaustive 'however, it is mainly Full HR Services and the Employee Lifecycle for your business. This also includes Learning and Development, Training, Employment Relations, and Employment Law within the Operational Setting. Recruitment, Resourcing and Retention along with Tailored Executive Coaching to unlock full potential and specialised training delivery are popular offerings. Our ethos is that "one size does not fit all" therefore, it is imperative that our offerings are bespoke for your business.

Our clients enjoy working with Chrystal HR & Coaching collaboratively and I ensure their needs and wants are met. They like drama-free HR, strong communication, and the diversion of people challenges to allow them and their business to grow and focus on managing their business.

During 2023, Chrystal HR & Coaching were involved in a number of key events from Entrepreneurial Woman and Business of the Year 2023. Woman Leadership Panel for Scottish Woman in Business to the Glasgow Chamber of Commerce International Woman's Day Event.

So why this book and why now? A commodity we cannot buy is time, why put off something until tomorrow that you could do today. Well, this book will do just that. It will expand your thoughts on 'what you think you know about HR' before it is too late.

Is it for business or just fun with a twist? Using my HR people experiences and anecdotal evidence (of course with some Poetic Licence to protect confidentiality) we will explore the unwritten world of HR.

During my career I have encountered some amazing people as well as some equally baffling characters. Therefore, I suspect that some of my readers may be reading the book just to see if they fall into the former or latter character buckets. It could transpire that success may look like less of "who I know" but "who knows me!"

Could this be my dynamic selling strategy? Are all my contacts and connections considered "Under Poetic Licence" and that's just for starters! Could they be the characters in this book, remember an HR Book isn't just for Christmas! It's all year round 24/7, spinning at 360 degrees.

However, before we get carried away, some of the contents of this book pushes the boundaries of the traditional HR to the point you could not make this stuff up! And at the end of the day, we are all Human and we shall Remain!

Enjoy the read!

Human Resources not Human Remains

Lose your dream,
you lose your mind.
You can't always get
what you want, but
if you try sometimes,
you might find you
get what you need.

- Rolling Stones

CHAPTER 1
ROLE

LET ME BE CLEAR, THIS IS HOW WE ROLE!

Tracey Chrystal

I t's winter on a dreich and cold morning on the southside of Glasgow. The HR team are busy and looking around my office is just like the bottom of a teenagers' wardrobe. Why Head Office persists on sending boxes of magazines whilst we have redundant forests which are full of dead trees is peculiar. Bundles of brochures for last month's staff engagement survey that we will now never need, and very little items of necessity is mind blowing. Based on our current safety record, posters on "what doesn't kill you makes you stronger" would even be better. When unpacked I'll check if this can be fitted together like a jigsaw or aligning remotely with the current HR Plan (now Version 7 to be precise) of Quarter 1.

Suddenly, the door flies open and a very sweaty out-of-breath bear from Operations crash lands in the office. The dramatic entrance left him dishevelled with beads of sweat running down his forehead as he blurted out....

"Morning" he says "Eh, eh, CID have arrived, and they need to speak with a senior human actually I have no idea who they want to speak with, can you help?" As I stood there in my Saville Row suit, hosting accessories of a designer high Vis vest and safety shoes that looked like I was Minnie Mouse on Tour. A very tall, cool, and calm gentleman appeared, looked me up and down from head to toe and clearly didn't rate the chick in the suit, even though the Top Cat name was now visible on the door. He swiftly advised "There is a problem" it sounded like "there's been a murder" whilst Mr Operations rolled his eyes as if he were naval gazing the room.

In that moment I had a flashback of being that young, masked female personnel advisor who progressed quickly along the then male-dominated career ladder, although the ratio of males to females in HR still remain a challenge today. I found myself falling backwards to my early days of the Trade Unions where my success grew upon the principle of learning and understanding pretty much everything like a sponge, especially negotiation techniques whilst letting a full delegation of male colleagues believe I was just this young girl from Personnel! Oh, how wrong they were when I took my mask off.

Back in the room another chap had arrived, and, in a heartbeat, I replied, "Good morning, gentlemen, how can I help?"

In my mind I immediately thought – this one is going to be a rollercoaster so everyone should strap in as this Gal ain't for turning!

You see I had worked for some of the most amazing and outstanding leaders for many years and experience tells you that situations like this are either 1-10 scenarios or a Defcon – in this case a Defcon 5! I could sense what was to come would require a Rock-solid approach and that pretty much summed me up.

Experience is an amazing learning path, your gut instinct: how you feel, and what you're going to say and do, don't come from a training course or learning book, the raw challenges are often managed from your own toolbox kit of skills and experience.

The need for the HR profession to be confidential whilst being fair, transparent, and not always leading by gut instinct? is essential but tough in many situations. To be clear CID (the Criminal Investigations Department) aiming to speak with HR means the theme is deception, loss, theft, or murder.

What became remarkable from that day forth was the sheer magnitude of what was bubbling over. Fact – we don't train the HR Management Students to solve crime in the community or amongst employees. We teach out at University, College and in the Workplace how to manage investigations, grievance, disciplinary, appeals, mock employment tribunals, arbitration, and negotiation with ACAS. Preparing for employment tribunal and yes, you have probably guessed by now that the next 6 months were going to feature using both my employment relations and employment law capabilities in the operational setting within a landscape that was even unique to me, this time round.

Surprisingly working in West Virginia, San Diego USA, India, Norway, Switzerland, Ireland and pretty much most of the UK, my senses were telling me one thing "Stay Calm." This is a strong trait when you are facing colleagues who are clearly wriggling around like a box of snakes. Indeed they were a band of thieves in disguise.

One piece of advice I would give where you can't always see the wood for the trees with widely different views and perspectives of how to fix something that's clearly wrong, is go back to what you learned in your studies about different personalities and behaviours. Like the Mr Men characters a name is useful, however the behaviour is important. In the box of snakes do you have the Hurry Up or the

Be Perfect, where did Mr Strong go and is the Pleaser of the group the ringleader! The truth was it became like a murder mystery until the game was over and when the clock stopped, and my head space was clear it was my turn to lift up the gauntlet.

What did we actually train our people? In this case, training was essential for the teams to fulfil tasks and activities of the day job. It was like a regimented military operation - deviating from how we have trained teams to carry out a process or procedure was breaching the defined process and daily instruction of work. As I looked around at very angry managers like a mob of frustrated wilder beasts, I found the need to raise my voice in the unfolding chaos and squawked, "Let me be clear this is how we will role – "get me the training records and get me them now."

The chick in the suit was back in the room, no longer that young personnel gal and this time no mask was required.

CHAPTER 2

JD

LEAVE THE JOB DESCRIPTION AT THE DOOR!

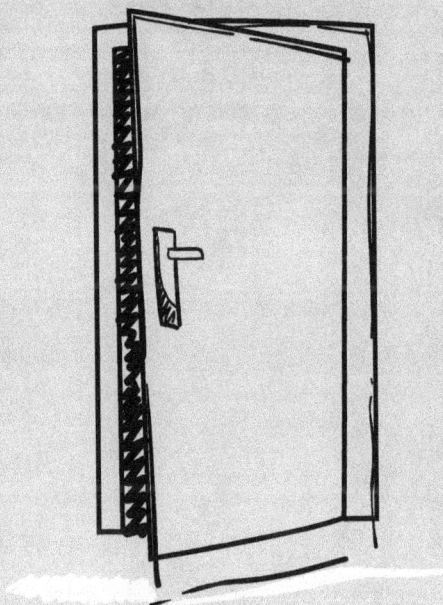

" Happiness often sneaks in through a door you didn't know you left opened.

- John Barrymore, American Actor "

Someone once told me, why have a dog and bark yourself.

Pondering over this statement, as my mind drifts to long weeks, sunny days, and designer pooch wear; harsh reality kicks in as I have never owned a dog, nor can I bark!

However, if I ever became a muddy-dog walking partner hygienically sweeping up poo with my poop bag (when the dog walker was unavailable), that at times may not be far off what HR need to cover and shovel on occasions. As many of my colleagues know a dachshund would be my dream choice. This is not because of the decades in HR of folks with muscular-skeletal challenges or in plain English, mainly chancers with bad-back syndrome.

But the idea made me reflect on some learning from the last year, a new approach – Killer Thinking. If you haven't yet heard of this, then here comes the training for today. "Killer Thinking," highly linked to solving everyday challenges is about being impactful, straightforward, loved, lasting support and respected. Pressing the buttons on emotional intelligence is revolutionising "wellbeing" and being radically transparent, "where bigger is not always better." As my thoughts drift again like an inflatable gliding in a swimming pool, maybe a little four-legged friend might be the tonic after all!

Killer Thinking, in plain English is to get to the root of the matter and point quickly: be open and honest while being your authentic self, breakdown the components into its small pieces, just like a job description to help find the best outcomes for you and others remembering to always place your oxygen mask on first before anyone else's.

Whilst the idea is of a new way of thinking, dog tails are bounced around in my head. A great friend and HR Colleague advised me "Christ Tracey, you don't have time for a dog, matter of fact you and I don't have time for a dog – goodness I'd leave to travel for work on a Monday and forget to feed the poor thing and it would be over the rainbow by Friday!"

In the moment, she was so right and making it clear to be a dog owner, you need a job description. Although we could both carve up a premium Job Description to suit, it doesn't mean that we have the skillset to manage DJ Dashshund.

As my writing colleague repeatedly reminds me "You're selling the sizzle honi, not the sausage" This ain't like writing HR Policy. And on that note, as I danced on the head of a pin about barking dogs, it was time to leave my "furry friends" behind and focus on one of the rudiments of HR – the Job Description (JD)!

At best this can highlight the tasks, activities, skills, and experience of a role. At worse it becomes a tick box exercise for another body in a seat and on the books. As I reflect on my career over the decades it was once acceptable to "label people" which is a horrid phrase.

It reminds me of crime dramas on the TV where the recently deceased appears in the morgue with a label attached to their hoof/claw/toe/digit. But as we are no longer living in the mid-70s, to think of people in this way is not acceptable, they're not just a number or a barcode.

The reverse of this scenario is not perfect either, the pendulum has swung further over the years than expected and this has an impact on the people we employ. For example: if you work for any company in the defence sector. On many occasions you must be a UK National – the amount of times companies are criticised for this is unbelievable and guess what? "They don't make the rules" and neither do HR. This is clear and factual. To this end HR can objectively justify this type of requirement. However, for everything else which lives like "particles in the ether," HR needs to get more scientific. Businesses need "can do people" more than ever.

This can no longer be like a pick-and-mix from Woolworths of skills whilst we sink like jellybeans in a bowl over political correctness and find ourselves dealing with the same issues each day. Its just different wallpaper, with no two days being the same.

During 2020 a pivotal change occurred.

For years HR Job Descriptions clearly stated, "must be able to travel" Why?

Because tradition insisted, we needed to be face-to-face in the room to deliver bad or good news!

This changed overnight. Endless team calls, who had ever heard of Zoom, sounded like a kids cartoon character. Little did we know we would be zooming, zipping, and zigzagging forever, shared screens, PDF documents, pausing and adjourning on screen whilst folks were ecstatic or weeping over furlough.

Whilst repeating the key 3 words "You're on Mute! ...."

The truth was HR sounded like a coffee advert – "From our kitchen and dining-room tables across the land we try every day to save jobs, at times irrespective of the job descriptions. Offices and sites remained closed and the Global HR community irrespective of their Job Descriptions adapted and this time this changed to "must NOT travel."

Let's continue to build on thinking "out of the box" and for the very last time the World of Work 2020.

Once the pandora's box lid is lifted, it never truly closes again. Once we peeked inside and outside and finally left the bizarre and remote stay-at-home mode, HR was faced with peculiar behaviours from the sublime to the ridiculous and throwing mindfulness into a Wednesday lunch! It was very clear some folks had forgotten their job description in its entirety, they clearly left this at the front door. There will be more discussion of this in Chapter 6 – The Little Book of HR Truths.

HR is not for the faint hearted.

My clients enjoy the benefits of working with me as a no-nonsense gal, accepting No Drama and focusing on the facts. My mantra is "leave the job description at the door"

Why?

- Because you have made the cut
- You are through the door
- You got the job!

However, for anyone who believes that simply sticking to the Job Description will get them far – then think again! Why?

Because the Job Description is simply like a recipe. Like making a cake, you have all the ingredients of what is needed for the job mix, however you need to have the skills, talent, and confidence to "bake the cake" and bring the job to life.

Hints and Tips for getting beyond the Job Description

1 Never ask anyone to do something you wouldn't do yourself.

2 Learn to make tea and coffee and get the Café order right – understand the kettle rules of FILL OR NO FILL.

3 Remember milk is not required in flavoured tea or you'll produce something resembling a "not so pleasant hot smoothie."

4 Smile and be positive as much as possible.

5 This is not a request "Keep your area tidy, it's called being mannerly. This isn't your turf yet, so for all the Millennials and Gen Zs consider the Gen X approach of collecting your own rubbish "– Quote Wombles, Children's TV Programme, 1968.

Well, maybe your get out of jail free card, is you were not born then.

6 Find the DNA of the business. What makes the place tick, follow the drumbeat of the business, or get back on the job search.

7 Dress for the job you want not the job you are in. Don't be confused by "Smart Casual" focus on the "Smart" in casual and less on the casual.

8 If the Job Description states commitment to out-of-hours working, or travel required. Then take the Rose-Tinted glasses off, as this ain't changing when probation ends.

9 Do the work, don't waste time, get on with it.

10 Be practical. **Success** is not a theory.

"You can't change your fate, but you can change your attitude.

- JM Barrie,
(Character - Tinkerbell)

CHAPTER 3
PRINCESSES

NO ROOM FOR PRINCESSES

The world of HR has changed.

Having a "passion" for the profession just doesn't cut it anymore.

Many dynamic HR professionals, worked from the bottom up. However, many realised quickly that understanding the "Bread & Butter" of HR involves much more.

Getting your hands dirty in all the places of the past that graduates have endured, such as supporting payroll, continuous minutes, pre-2000s trade unions and disciplinaries of hairy butt fitters and watching grown men cry are all long gone. The challenge nowadays, if you are not covering this type of stuff "No bum cracks here" then you will pigeonhole yourself in the glamorous world of HR. When you truly find your whole self in this place "prince's included" then please call me!

Or am I just dreaming like Blondie!

So, continuing on the theme of "glamorous," job titles can be very attractive but lack substance.

When I was a graduate, we didn't have "Specialised-Talent Acquisition Directors" or "Employee Engagement Entrepreneurial Executives" which nowadays is great although if the business changes, you're hardly helicoptering into a Head of People, Director of Wellbeing or Group HR Director role. As they all have very different job descriptions.

In the spirit of HR teamwork "we need to get stuff done" whatever the specialism and this is more often than not where you'll find your very own "Prize Princess" lurking in the team. Fabulous at organising the best swanky bars, restaurants, and clubs for all Team Social events, but completely useless at any flying solo form of HR Delivery, let alone reporting correlations or going above and beyond the HR role!

When you peel back how this glamorous gal joined the team more often than not referred, sometimes on the cusp of nepotism in a time when someone needed to fill a gap. The problem is no one ever managed the gap and she still remains flying the flag for HR and Harvey Nicks! This is a polished way of fitting a round peg in a square hole.

Let's be clear, I am a huge advocate for polished people. The one truth that is often ignored in HR is everybody from time to time looks at your mits and talons. Why?

You are often in charge of their destiny in that meeting moment of figure work – salary benefits, redundancy, settlement, or retirement are important to people, and they often get nervous.

Reading their body language is helpful, however it is often human nature that when you look down to explain figures they look down as well. Therefore, if you have been gardening or painting the day before, it's best to avoid those types of interactions or have your talons tamed to meet the world.

Managing Princesses in your team can be derailed if they also learned tantrums and traits from mixed behaviours from HR Directors (HRDs). However, it is comforting to note that although they can't change their fate, they can change their attitudes, both Princesses and HRDs alike who came through the same rank.

In my experience rogue HRDs fall into two categories which they can toggle between in a nano second. "Cruella de Vil to Mary Poppins" or "Cinderella." This is an opportunity to learn how "NOT TO DO SOMETHING."

If this book helps it should influence the industry about when this pendulum- swing behaviour between the clear characters exists; aka going from The Villian to Practically Perfect in every way. HR needs to hold individuals accountable for this type of behaviour as the ambiguous approach is killing our HR Team comradery.

Let's unpack this a little.

It's Spring in London, the sun is shining and there is not a cloud in the sky. As the plane arrives at the terminal outside it looks like Summer. The windsocks on the tarmac are not even moving from their placement. A train ride via the Bank Line and the heart of the city beats as it does pretty much 24/7. This is going to be a great day. Or so I thought!

Everyone had put their heart and souls in the new business stream opening and for HR, 5 months of structure changes to achieve our best people where available to take on a new and shiny entity.

Lines and lines of project plans were completed and closed out like the last hour in a patisserie when there is nothing left to sell. Today would allow life to go back to normal for many, and for me allow a return to another day of my weekly diary without a 4am start. As I approached the office the concierge looked rather down beat. "Good morning, Claude." He looked at me and said "Morning TC, but this ain't going to be a good one! 'Devil wears Prada' is here and she launched through that elevator like a Rhino!" (and he didn't mean hippo (high potential), He meant the loose wild Rhino running towards your cyber security policy), as he swung his head quickly to the right.

I looked over at the elevator and noticed it had stopped on the 15th floor. "Oh, thanks Claude. I'll get my head gear on." As I pressed the shiny green upwards arrow of the lift, my head space was full. What explosion awaited me this morning, and how much damage had been done before I even entered the room.

As the lift moved, I felt the g-force race to the 15th floor so fast I couldn't even focus on the sun's reflection on the many glass buildings as I laboured with my thoughts. The doors opened and the 'circus had already been unleashed.'

Many of the team were running around like players in a game of rounders.

There was a lot of noise, and the newest member of the HR team was crying with her head in her hands. "Cruella de Vil" was thumping the table and bellowing through what was 'supposed' to be soundproof glass offices!

As my HR Project Manager ran towards me like a bowling ball bouncing and missing a strike, gasping for breath she blurted out – in a tone that only cats and dogs may understand.

I responded calmly "Amy, slow down, what is the problem?"

She responded, "Alana is not happy with page 4 of the new entity publication advert and she doesn't like the colour of the signage".

"Ok get the proofs and signatures – she signed off everything except the final signage. I'll deal with that and Amy – slow down and breathe, along with 2 low-fat lattes – no sweeteners."

As I walked closer to the glass box office Alana's eyes fixed on mine and she quickly dismissed another crying crew member from the room. We need to stay calm and afloat although Captain Jack aka Alana Jack was single handedly sinking the ship! As I pushed the heavy glass door opened and it closed behind me like walking into a freezer with powerful suction of an interplanetary craft. This was it, Showtime.

"Good morning, Alana."

"Don't 'Good Morning' me, I employed you because I thought you had more than a few brain cells, what do you expect our clients will say about that colour?"

I replied in a very deep and sarcastic tone "Let me think – it's lime! The same colour as in our hiring campaign."

"Yes, lime/green it is. I don't like green, I've never liked green, we are not having green!"

I tried to explain "Ok, firstly it blends with the pool blue turquoise and secondly, the design team advised that it would give our corporate clients a sense of space. Let alone it's a strong 'we care about the environment colour.'

"So, what!" she replied as she gritted her teeth like the Wolf of Wall Street.

This behaviour was regular.

Cruella would get even more angrier if she would understand the logic and guess what? that understanding usually followed with the post-tantrum dance of 'ok this might just work'.

Note to self: in 2 weeks time she will claim the credit for all of this.

In that second Amy trying to master the freezer door appeared with files under one arm and two skinny lattes in the other. "Thanks Amy" I said as she managed the door with as little grace and ease as I did, before scurrying away like a rat on a sinking ship.

"Let's have a seat and a coffee" I said to Alana like I was the more senior one in the room.

She grabbed a pen from the desk and started playing with it as if she were smoking a cigarette along with the coffee. As she was a reformed smoker the action usually calmed her down like a screaming little person on a flight, when the Calpol or Nurofen kicks in.

"Here are the approval sheets Alana. The brochure and advert proofs were signed by you." She snatched the poly pockets from my hand shaking her head from side to side like a little person refusing to have a hat on. "Mmmm, the glossy content and the advert look different on the finished copy" she said as she shook the pen around as if it was an old-fashioned cigarette holder.

"They might look different in the glossy materials and wide screen advert, but the 'content' is the same," I responded. She was finally boxed in with nowhere else to go.

In a heartbeat she pushed herself back on the wheels of her chair like a rollercoaster ride preparing for warp speed. "Fine we will work with this, but you my gal need to improve your colour palette!" replied the woman who only 6 weeks ago had told me she didn't care what damn colour anything was. It could be purple with pink polka dots for all she cared, and this attitude extended to who we recruited.

I smiled and proceeded to watch her swing this hideous door open until it actually wedged itself ajar.

Post-Tantrum Cruella hovered over the office and thrust her hand in the air whilst shouting "Get those damn cakes out of here I am on a diet!"

"Fine" said my colleague Lucy in a little squeaky mouse tone "apologies it's my 30th birthday".

Like a ballerina on pointe Cruella spun round and to everyone's relief said "Oh Lucy how lovely" as she grinned like a Cheshire Cat. Yep, she was morphing into Cinderella.

At that moment, the office felt more like a panto than Corporate HR. As I stepped out of the glass office box I stated again "Morning."

Let's remember team we can't always change our fate, but we can change our attitudes. As the day continued my mind shifted to the HR Job Description again.

Next time let's have more psychologist and peacemaker traits!

Next minute there was a bellow from the reception. Yes, you guessed it, Cinderella had once again morphed back to Cruella in a nano second. "Stress balls, 'Lime' stress balls" Cruella screamed, and we were back in the Pantomime.

DRAMA

NO DRAMA

REALLY!

CHAPTER 4
BOARD ROOM

THE PAINT IS THE SAME COLOUR ON THE OTHER SIDE OF THE DOOR

> **66**
>
> Don't spend time
> beating on a wall
> hoping to transform
> it into a door.
>
> — Coco Chanel
>
> **99**

CHAPTER

4

BOARD
ROOM

T

he Boardroom

For many folks this means two things, either A: they have just sat down to watch the UK or the USA 'The Apprentice,' or B: The Board Meeting is this week!

The first immediately reminds me of a nice cold glass of wine, relaxing on the sofa with scooby snacks whilst I spend the next hour shouting at the TV.

However, the latter for many will be approximately 4 hours of your life that from time to time you will never get back, or would you want to?

It can be a strange place, the Boardroom. Many times, it is where the unrecorded conversations take place, followed by a hot bed of gossip like "Nicole, did you see James being taken into the Boardroom? Bet that's him caught with his expenses scam? "What," or "Oh, there is a lot of folks in there today and it's not a Board meeting!"

"I knew there was something going on when Jamie did not get that job in Audit... no point giving folks new jobs if we can't fill the old ones when we are all for the high jump".

Or, "that's that girl from marketing finally reporting that creep in IT. Wouldn't it make you shudder just thinking about it. Oh, and Occupational Health are there as well!"

When the 'hot bed of gossip' occurs, HR are usually the crew that find out about it last. As it comes from the grapevine, this isn't usually factual or correct as no complaint ever arrives.

So, let's consider the possibilities of this gossip as people usually make this stuff up. No drama!

Examples:

1 James wants to ask a private question about referring a colleague he knew from another firm.

2 IT need to discuss some new software and have invited a couple of developers and team contacts in for a review.

3 The marketing gal is looking to speak to HR and Occupational Health regarding an up-and-coming new Health and Wellbeing in the workplace video as maybe we should consider mindfulness to help prevent paranoia setting in!

However, whether gossip, meeting or Non-Exec Board Director duties over the years, Boardrooms have been mysterious places sometimes for all the wrong reasons.

For Senior HR Professionals reading this chapter, you will know all too well that it can be nerve-wracking when you are presenting at Board. You review your documents and presentation, over and over again, like you are auditioning for a West End show.

My advice is ensure you know who your allies are before you step into the room. This is not to be unlawful, but to understand if this all goes pear-shape, that you will have someone to help bring the tribe back to the table, or should we read bribe. No!

As you wait to find out your slot, praying like the Italian Vatican, "Please let this be before lunch."

The deadly graveyard shift is a real killer and most of us have been there.

Once you are actually in there, you're not sure whether to cough loudly, so as to wake up the old codger, or scan the room like a Dalek asking questions on the subject matter.

The only risk on the latter, the subject matter, is you!

As the day arrives you end up sitting outside the Boardroom waiting to be summoned. You stare at the wall, the floor and nod endlessly at those relaxed employees who walk past thinking "Poor sod, glad that's not me." As you sit longer it becomes like a dentist waiting room. Eventually the door opens, and a friendly, but flushed face appears with those dreaded words, "Hi Tracey, so sorry we are running late on the financial projections. Could you be a dear and grab a coffee and we'll be ready for you in an hour." French Connection UK (FCUK)! I could be Human Remains in an hour not bloody Human Resources.

Although at this point you feel physically sick, you smile calmly, and say "Absolutely, no problem. "Thank You." No bloody drama.

As you get up to walk away, your legs don't really work. Pins and needles run down your calves as if you have jumped into ice cold water, because you have been sitting so long, with no need to explain what part of your anatomy has gone numb.

As you breathe in through your nose, and out through your mouth, you walk stiltedly along the corridor to the café area. Although you appear cool, calm, and collected, you're waddling along the corridor like a tiny duck paddling frantically 100 times faster under the water.

After 45 minutes, a coffee, some fresh air and a visit to the restroom, you return to the dentist's waiting room chair. This time as you sit, you can actually see the wall, the floor, and the Boardroom door, praying once again for this to go well and be over.

As you sit there, a voice comes into your head, "Hey, it's not that bad, like nobody has died, no human remains or anything worse." The dark-green Board door suddenly opens and startles you and you begin to shake like a leaf. Then a voice from nowhere says "Board are ready for you now!."

After a decade of being on the other side of the Board Room door, where invariably the paint is the same colour, an opportunity presented itself. In early 2017, I applied to be considered for a Non-Exec Board Directors role.

This was a real thrill for me, a Board Director. Could the glass-ceiling effect finally be conquered?

My presentation for interview was like preparing 100 times over for Board. What would I wear? How would I clear my diary or even take the day off? Anyway, this was happening. I was absolutely ready to push that green Board door open.

What I didn't realise, even being interviewed by an all-male panel, was that if successful, I would join an all-male Board.

Somehow, this surprised me as the Boardrooms that I was used to had all mixed Boards. However, having grown up with the Trade Unions in the mid-80s, an all-male dominated environment was the least of your worries.

What legal stuff did I need to know? Would this shiny-new opportunity carry any personal or financial risk? Would I be taken seriously, or would I be seen as the token female? All these thoughts were very soon squashed when my offer letter arrived, and at that point, I was through the door, high heels clicking on the wooden floor.

Initially, my girlfriends were confused. My thoughts were 'let's not do shots' and control our 'socials' both became the forefront on my mind. Although on reflection, my career was based on a discipline of "work hard, play hard," the champagne bubbles were never far from the top. Being a Board Director was not going to change that!.

The best business suit I ever bought was the most expensive and even a size bigger just to ensure I looked amazing! Stilettos that high, made me feel like being on top of the Eiffel Tower with all the sparkling lights beneath me. The Boardroom below felt weird and eerie. It felt so different from popping in and out for a quiet conversation to being the full Boardroom which resembled the Super Bowl!

The table, the chairs and wall art look huge, expensive and very different from before. All in all, it felt like a very lonely place. However, when you are there in the moment, regardless of being alone you have made it, to the Boardroom.

Success is often a very lonely place if you let it be so. Or you can think like the "Circus Master" in the Ring. This is your chance to have influence. As my thoughts flipped from positive to negative it felt like the angel flipped to the devil on my shoulder. Suddenly the Boardroom filled and I am now formally in the Old Boys Club. I am no longer that young chick from personnel although I wasn't that young anymore!

Watching people behaviours, sketching board paper sections for pensions and resource issues was suddenly reality. My class act was established "Noses in Fingers Out." What this means is no room for twaddle, gossip, rumours or operational challenges. The razor-sharp focus needs to be oversight, governance, and compliance. This is now a legendary statement for Non-Executive Board Directors and just like a bullet train this trip was not stopping any time soon.

Weeks, months and even years passed. I was elevated from being the token female to being "Witch of the West." Finally, I realised when sitting in the corridor on the other side of the green door, that Senior HR Professional thinking was actually really important stuff.

It was when it hit me. Like the crazy-rugby mother that I was, the challenge on the other side of the door was no different than inside the Boardroom. It may have been a different day, different outfit, and a different pair of stilettos, but the wallpaper was just the same. My work here was going to take a while. In fact, it took several years to be precise.

I rose from the "HR Warrior" to the "Chosen Female" to the "Chick that got things done!." Regardless, I was still someone who needs to work on her time management. As I was simply doing too much. I was repeatedly wearing my pants on the outside of my trousers just like a female super NE.

Aka, Non-Executive Director extra or dinar.

> " Be the woman
> who fixes another
> woman's crown
> without telling
> the world it was
> crooked. "
>
> - Amy Morin

CHAPTER 5

CROWN

STRENGTHEN THE CROWN

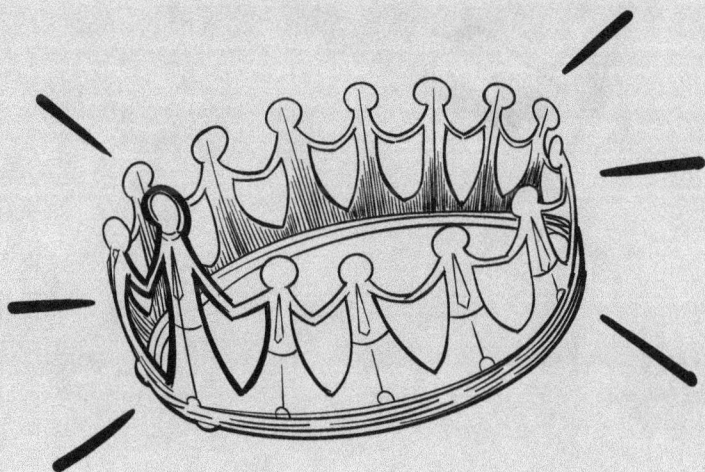

Women in Leadership or Women Rewriting the Narrative – that is the question?

"Whether it is nobler in the mind to suffer the slings and arrows of outrageous fortune, or to take arms against a sea of troubles, and by opposing end them." I knew that one day I would need to remember that speech from Hamlet, that I remember from Higher English.

Shakespeare aside, decades of psychological research confirm that when women are empowered to take on leadership positions, the effect can be metamorphic for everyone. Women are more likely to encourage what is good in an organisation, and better inspire people to go along with its mission when compared to men.

It is widely known that team collaboration is greatly inspired by the presence of women in the group. Group-collective intelligence is stronger with their ability to work together and solve a wider range of problems.

Hiring female CEOs and Board Directors has been associated with changes in an organisation's use of language by helping to associate women with characteristics that are critical for leadership success.

Here I believe there are 3 key messages:

① Absolute integrity in everything

② Everything in moderation

③ Hire the right people and get out of their way.

We should always strive to do the right thing and to do our best to live with integrity. I believe integrity is doing the right thing when no one is watching.

Getting a seat at the Boardroom table is not enough. The time is now for more women at the head of the table in all leadership roles.

My unquestionable ethos of being a qualified executive coach and mentor is helping other women understand their worth and I help them find their courage to empower them to lead from a place of confidence and strength.

As an executive coach I see beyond my client's limits and my purpose is to guide them to greater things. I help ensure that they know what good looks like and never forget it. I work with them so they are able to acknowledge and share their knowledge and experiences. I believe if you see someone struggling then you help them.

I would always send the "career ladder of success" back down as there will be undoubtedly another female finding her feet. While climbing this career ladder of success she will no doubt be juggling multiple tasks from work to home to family and even to studies.

So, what are the rules of SUCCESS? First of all – embrace failure...

Failures are simply stepping stones on your path to greatness. Embrace them as wonderful opportunities to learn, grow and evolve.

So, what do we mean when we say, 'Fixing the Crown?' It is very simply recognising the female intrinsic value and encouraging them to show up with their full self in every situation.

In a quote by JM Barrie from his character Tinkerbell remember "Think happy thoughts and you will fly."

So here is the learning part for today!

Below are outlined the **Do's** and **Don'ts** of Leadership:

PS those of us in the HR industry will know that nothing is ever just equal and opposite. Those eagle-eyed individuals who think I have missed half the table can relax.

DO's	DON'Ts
Active Listening	Poor Listening skills
Accountability	No Accountability
Adaptability	Poor adaptability skills
Clear Vision	Unclear Vision
Constant Approach	Inconsistency
Decision-making	Inability to make tough decisions
Delegation	No entrustment
Empathy	No Empathy
Encouraging people development	Overlooking development of people
Fair approach	Favouritism
Integrity	No integrity
Proper Communication	Improper or Unacceptable Communication
Recognition of Team Efforts	Failure to recognise and reward employees
Self-Awareness	No Self Awareness
Willingness to take Calculated Risk	Lack of Risk Appetite
	Decisions based on emotions or biases
	Causing emotional stress
	Creating Drama

This focus is that it takes more effort not to do something right, or just simply in the wrong way, than it does to get it right in the first place.

Like 'Chloe in Marketing' taking longer to tell you how she can't do something than the time it would have taken her to do it.

Or in comparison, 'cool and collective Cara' who always starts her explanation with "This is not an excuse, it's a reason"

Remember 'Salt and Sugar' technically look the same but taste different! Therefore, whether you have a 'Chole' or a 'Cara' or even a 'Colin the Caterpillar,' lookout for the different approaches.

Here are some fun facts about female leadership in the Boardroom.

1. Ensure your underwear and waist bands are comfy as you are going to be sitting there a long time, and they will expand.

2. Remember if you take your heels off under the table they will need to go back on at some point.

3. Don't be distracted by anyone when a comfort break is called, Time is precious and there may be a queue for the loo.

4. Take no prisoners. If referred to at any time by male colleagues as a woman, female or newbie reply as a proud board director. I shall reply to your comment in my head whilst screaming 'The Bitch is Back' by Elton John in my head.

5. Prepare, Prepare, and Prepare – avoid paper and killing trees. Take an iPad or laptop, showing up as an eco-warrior. Make cryptic notes.

6. Don't eat all the sandwiches and cakes even if they are tempting. It looks so unladylike. As the older you get, the longer it will take to work off the carbs.

But most of all enjoy yourself, you deserve to be there.

What about – The revolution has started. Let's smash that glass ceiling. Emerge as the queen bee.

"People who are
wrapped up
in themselves
make small
packages.

- Benjamin Franklin

CHAPTER 6
TRUTH
LITTLE BOOK OF
HR TRUTHS

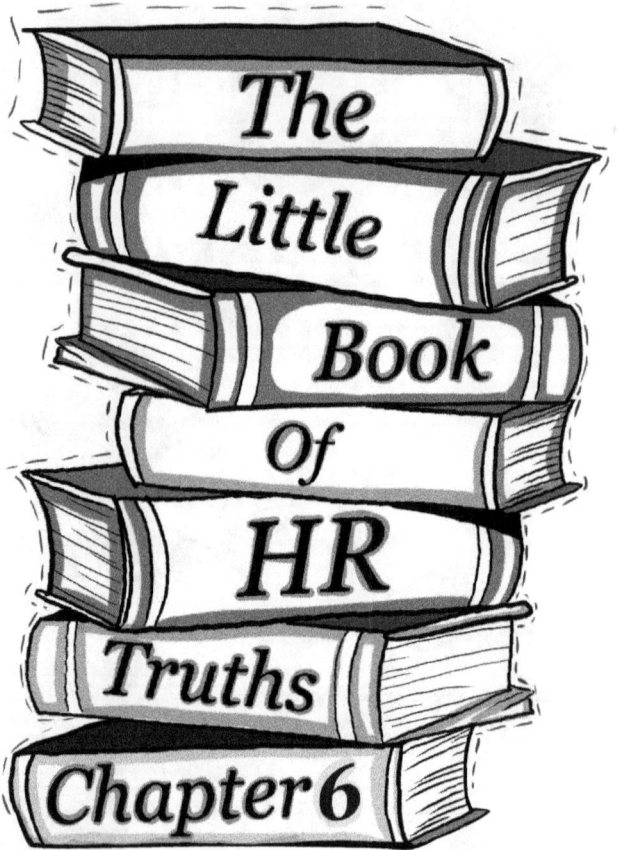

The
Little
Book
Of
HR
Truths
Chapter 6

The time is right for sex, or simply just the sexy stuff. No holding back here...it's about to get juicy.

So, are we going to hear the sexy and juicy stuff? Yes, we are indeed.

Cast your mind back to the job description (JD) and folks forgetting their own JD in its entirety. So, what was one of the other side effects of the 2020 pandemic ... memory loss! Despite having detailed JD's people decided to make up the content as they went along.

The world was a weird place back then in 2020. Much as we can laugh about it now, at the time it was earthshattering!

I remember standing there thinking I could really do with a decent drink but realising the necessity of the day was keep a safe distance so that was never going to happen any time soon.

Whilst everyone was trying to keep 2 meters apart, how could you possibly have any physical contact, when you had to keep at least 6 feet apart? The working practice was to keep everyone safe, to prevent contact to prevent the spread of disease. Safe working practices could not have been more difficult with no physical contact and nobody walking around with a measuring tape in their back pocket. Well, we did paint the floors which are now an indelible memory imprinted on my brain.

A statement that will undoubtedly stay with me forever during the pandemic was "look, it's quite simple. If you don't have a cough and you can stick a pickle in your mouth, and smell it and taste it – then you are fine!"

WTF was that? That was not how we were going to roll. Just to be clear "no pickles were required". The world loves a trier, but this wasn't going to happen.

Oh, and one of those other haunting memories that will never be exorcised, will be the day I opened a large cupboard in Facilities. A couple, as they say in the Malteser's advert were getting it on or just being jiggy amongst the dusters and brooms. My reaction as a human being, not as a HR Director, was OMG. If I shut the door quickly, will they think I never saw them? to "Shut the Door Quickly." Or even worse, will it get rid of that sight, indelible on my brain. The problem was they recognised me, but even worse I recognised the coupling couple.

How many times have you heard the saying "How many folks from HR does it take to change a lightbulb?" ...and you thought that statement was only reserved for blondes (no disrespect! I am now one!!).

Well, let me tell you how many times over the years have HR had to tell folks, "can you please keep your bits, upper body and lower body parts, either or both at the same time, out of the photocopier." Just, like a zillion times, or maybe even more.

Then you get challenged for being a 'prude.' 'Prude' ... really! "It's a bloody health and safety risk mate."

So even without thinking, you roll your eyes so hard they almost go back into your head, you begin to think, I am like a person possessed. What am I doing here?

Talking about people being possessed, why am I even here? This takes me back to a really cold day in May and it was snowing when I was wearing sling backs and dressed to kill in the latest fashion of the day. Well, it had been reduced to a work dress because I had been on a first date and the "beau" in question thought I was a masseuse. So, I had clearly walked out and it became an immediate last date. I didn't even waste time exchanging business cards. Could this day get any better? Oh yes, trade unions.

Going into battle it is so necessary not to have any chinks in your armour. However, if your trade unions are angry, doesn't matter how much chainmail you command, and I am not talking about email chain mail!

Deep down they are still human beings, even if many of them think it's the 1970s with Arthur Scargill and the legendary combover hairstyle. Nowadays, balding men shave their head which in the 1970s, meant you were either an aging skinhead or a convict!

On one occasion, a 'helpful soul,' being the representative of a large group of workers, couldn't find his way into a glass meeting room. As HR, we are meant to be helpful, support, dialogue and facilitate negotiations. However, even this becomes difficult when a full-grown man, built like the proverbial (poetic licence claimed) brick sh!thouse, is waving his hands like a French Pierrot mime artist on the other side of the glass. His attempt to defeat the glass and find the meeting room door handle was highly amusing to say the least. Like all the other managers present, trying to stay professional, we were rooted to the spot to witness the entertainment. My muscles froze, and my mouth smiled blankly making me look just like a Tweenie – a CBBC lookalike. As I stared in disbelief, I thought, well this was going to be a cracker!

HR Staff Engagement and support goes from the sublime to the ridiculous.

I had a chap who would quietly come into my office, when I was on a call or video conference. His intention was always to "borrow" a box of picture and wall hooks.

The line of questioning was always the same:

"Do maintenance not provide these?"

"Apparently not unless we want to buy a million of them."

Honestly, it was like the Two Ronnie's Four Candles script. That memorable sketch, "The Hardware Shop" when Ronnie Corbet was playing the hardware shopkeeper who kept getting more and more frustrated. Ronnie Barker was the customer with a broad southern accent whose words were misinterpreted when trying to purchase handles, for forks confused with candles.

With an even broader Glaswegian accent your interpretation of the "hook" should remain silent and a bloody shovel in this case would have been even more useful.

The Top 10 Excuses for Anything and Everything:

1. My granny died. (I've often wondered how many grannies some staff had in their lifetime!)

2. My hamster ate through the Wi-Fi cable, that's why I couldn't upload the file earlier when working from home. (The updated version of the dog ate my homework.)

3. Yes, that main dish in the canteen was a bit dodgy today. I'm going to need to go home.

4. I didn't realise I needed a fit note.

5. My granny died. "What again" I ask. Oh, that's my other granny. (Even more grannies than the artful dodger.)

6. Can't find my ID badge and couldn't get into the building. (Really — how different is that from losing it.)

7. I think, I am coming down with what's been going around everyone. Seems to be a 24–48-hour thing. (Truthfully - see you in a few days.)

8. You didn't sign in for the monthly training set yesterday? 'I was too busy' (Honestly- 'I don't care.')

9. Yep, that report is just about finished. 'Really?' I respond, 'The last time I looked you were on page 4 of 18'.

10. Aw, I didn't notice that I had to give notice to leave, silly me. Bye. (Answers on a postcard.)

Strange things that Managers and Employees Say and Do!

- "Awe Tracey, so glad you are in just now, I need your advice. I'm going to need to go down to that bloody school again, canny take much more of this. She's only been sent home from school again for wearing white Converse. They say they are not suitable, even though they cost a bloody fortune."

  "Listen, not a problem, go deal with what you need to" I say, thinking that was an easy one. Mother of the Year looks at me pauses and says "Shoes! Shoes! That's not my problem, she is sitting beside someone who identifies as a Zebra!" In that moment I thought that I need to send Mother of the Year for more diversity training.

- "Yep, I've got it! We need a new job title that can cover everyone, say 100+ people?"

  "Ok, is that not the senior roles?" I reply tentatively.

  "Yes, but they are all specific roles – Head of Procurement, Head of Finance etc. this person would be a key people lead!"

  "Ok, what you thinking?" I say as I'm thinking someone is pinching my job.

"He could be called the Tsar!"

"Whit?? That's not even a scrabble word" I reply exasperated, with my hand on my forehead.

- "You know I am keen to have a family" ...and I'm thinking that's great he wants to be a dad when in the bad old days men would have thought another "wean" and mouth to feed.

"Yes of Course, I understand"

"Well, I need some help regarding Paternity Leave"

"Congratulations, I am delighted that the fertility treatment worked" and I am thinking silently thinking that was quick.

"No Tracey, you don't understand I am still attending the fertility clinic"

"Ok." I look at a washed up 35-year-old shipwreck standing in my office. I cannot believe I am actually asking this "So, who is the paternity leave for?"

"Aye, me, yeah me and the gal on the help desk"

In that moment, my advice to all junior and senior HR professionals is to FIND THE TECHICAL ANSWER AND SMILE.

You see all 3 adults in this Bermuda triangle were employees in the same company and even in the same building. Fertility leave and Paternity leave are all well and good under the Family Friendly Policy. However, in the case of Captain Shipwreck who had a First Mate and a Second First Mate a gale was imminent because one of his mates would undoubtably make him walk the plank.

Captain Shipwrecks choices were to have either Fertility leave or Paternity leave but not both. Pity he didn't have the same creative approach to the "mates" women in his life, or maybe he did.

"Oh, I didn't realise you couldn't have both... I mean the leave that is" he stammered, as he looked at me with a face as red as a red-port can but as its HR its as red as a Belisha beacon!

"That's ok" I reply. Captain Shipwreck looked as if he landed on the rocks and couldn't get away quick enough. "Let me know what you would like to do" I say in a bewildered and vague tone "... annual leave is also an option."

At that moment, my HR Advisor, Sam appears. Captain Shipwreck appears as if he is looking at Ursula, the human, mermaid, sea-witch villain, and the dance begins. She wants to enter and he wants to leave and I am thinking yet again, what is the technical answer here! "Sorry" he says as he skulks away with his tail between his legs. Sadly, he hadn't though the situation through before he ended up in his menage et trois.

"Samantha, close the door" I say in an authoritative voice. "Are you ok? You look a bit flustered."

"You are not going to believe this one," she says as her eyes light up like a Christmas tree "Bianca from the Service Desk is pregnant and Mr Shipwreck's the dad!" she blurts out.

"Yip" I reply in a discerning tone, and I wasn't even trying to get over the line first.

"Wait, you know?" she says, raising her eyebrows.

"Yip"

"But I thought he was having fertility tests with his wife from Purchasing?"

"Yip"

"Christ, is that why he was in here, to tell you this?"

"Yip, a real tag team effort. Fullmark's for approaching HR at the same time, no favourites there.

"Miss Service to you, Mr Shipwreck to me"

"What are you going to do?" she says flapping her arms.

They don't even teach this type of thing in the HR Management Level 3. In fact, they don't teach it at Level 5 or Level 7, or any level for that matter of fact.

"We are going to be super confidential as ever and treat this Bermuda triangle of employees with dignity and respect on whichever level or policy they need support with."

"And what if it gets out?" she asks tentatively.

"Well, it's not coming from us, or you'll be fired, and I'll be right out the door behind you? Remember Samantha it's not what we do, but how we do it"

Moving on, here are some 'Expressions' used by Management and HR

Eat your frog

Don't put off until tomorrow what you can do today.

A bird in the hand is worth two in the bush.

Don't recruit a hygienist when you need a dentist.

I want to pick my eyeballs out with cocktail sticks.

When in doubt "Absolutely" as a response normally works.

Every dog has its day.

If they had a brain, they would be dangerous.

The lights are on, but no one is in.

Not the sharpest tool in the shed.

Sandwich short of a picnic.

In one ear – out the other.

He/she will be the death of me.

For the love of God.

Rockets! The lot of them.

It's like herding cats.

She gave me that "Camel chewing sherbet look."

Like pushing an elephant up a hill.

Wading through the treacle.

Anyone can work hard

The elephant in the room.

There's a rhino and it's running right at you.

And finally....

The Christmas decorations were not yet down. The unfinished boxes of chocolates and the treats in the advent calendars were still lying around. These unfinished goodies will no longer be eaten due to the annual January, New Year resolution of "I'm on a diet.

Echoes along every corridor like the song sung by Dory in Nemo. Time and memorial say that these resolutions will only last until the 3rd week of January. Then, without admonishment, someone will crack, and with the least wee excuse, everyone falls off the wagon and everyone trots down to the pub after work.

January blues...

A surprised colleague Eddie appeared and said "I am in shock"

"Is everything alright?"

"No, not really"

"Well, let's sit down and chat"

"Ok, well you know that chap we interviewed pre-Christmas Andy, well he has just turned up as Alice."

"Alice? Have we got the right candidate?"

"Oh yes, his paperwork is accurate"

Interestingly as I spoke with Eddie, he seemed relieved that I was trying to be understanding. My thoughts are racing. We are going to need to change ID Badge, Records, Payroll, New Starter info which is fine although Eddies main concern was what loo would the gal use!

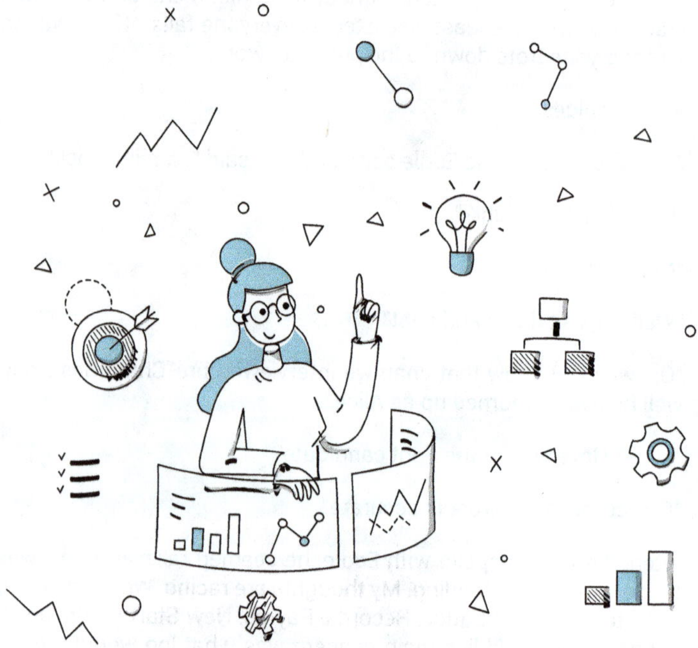

"

The irresistible
Top Cat and
leader of the
pack

- Hannah Barbera
Animation

"

CHAPTER 7
TOP CAT
TOP CAT TO BOSS CAT

Once you have mastered the craft of HR, then you are neither a novice, nor a guru just yet.

A strange phenomenon occurs.

Team dynamics kick in and, despite this, some delightful person is always further up the knowledge tree than the others.

This isn't always the planned path.

However, being one of the best at something, even if not HR related, is a particularly good thing. Now, this can be quite far reaching for someone like, let's say Jenny, who is the team baker. The glorified end-result is that we, the HR high heid-yins kill it on every Charity Coffee and Cake Day. We win hands down and we raise more cash than the office café.

Another phenomenon is the HR Groupie who knows everything musical. They are an authority on concerts, live bands, Glastonbury and even film. The result is hands-down winning every quiz so we end up with the best raffle prizes at every event.

However, on my journey of being Top Cat to Boss Cat, I had so many vertical learning experiences.

One that certainly took the biscuit was the day an HR Manager in my team proclaimed the most fabulous statement: "No Problem if Star Baker Jenny is off. I was HR Business Partner for all things Biscuit!"

My excitement and enthusiasm missed a key message there "ALL things biscuit."

Reminds me of earlier reminiscences where we see failures as stepping stones on our journey to greatness.

Only this time my stepping stone was a huge, long, long-jump... Literally!

The eventful day arrives. Everyone is covering their charity stations. HR are running a number of fun competitions along with Cake & Candy. Trust me, the standard was so high, that the eloquence of the displays could put Fortnum & Masons to shame.

As I am trotting along the corridor in my trainers. My usual footwear was high heels as trainers were simply not appropriate office footwear in those days. I was thinking, this is fabulous as I can move twice as fast. A gal at the 5th floor reception says, "aye the very person. Security are looking for you."

"No problem" I say as I exit sharp left and run into the elevator.

As I edge to the back of the elevator, clearly aware that this is a lift with a glass floor, as I am looking down at Security there not just eyeballing me.

As the lift is approaching the ground floor, I can clearly see a small gathering of the clans.

I skip out, my happy go lucky self, thinking it's just sports day. 'Our legend in all things that no one else knows about the building,' John, approaches me.

"Right Tracey, glad to see you. This delivery. What is it and where is it to go?"

As I look for the parcel, realise that the daylight at the whole glass front of the building is obliterated by a huge artic. John and I exchange the look, "well he's not entering the back lane."

"No problem, John. Do we know what's being delivered?"

"Aye, something big."

As John and I spin through the revolving glass door onto the street, indeed there is a 40-foot truck there and a lorry driver in the middle of an altercation with a traffic warden.

To my dismay she shouts over the engine noise "Right big fella, you've got 10 mins to get this monster truck shifted before I come back roun!".

Wow, a traffic warden with a heart. Usually, they look like a cross between the Tin Man from The Wizard of Oz or a Cyberman from Doctor Who. But she was the ultimate Rottweiler with lipstick.

"Thanks for waiting" I shout.

"Are you Crystal from HR?"

"Yes, I'm Tracey Chrystal."

"Can you sign here please?" as he sticks a clipboard and a pen in my face.

"Of course, but what am I signing for... exactly??"

He looks me up and down and says "... well biscuits of course!"

"Biscuits?" I say in shock.

"Yip."

I reply with a vague look. "How many exactly?"

"The full load."

"There must be some mistake, we were expecting a few boxes."

"Nope, you're having a full 40-tonne truck load, love!"

At that point I am scanning the delivery note to see if we are paying for this monster delivery of biscuits, which to my joy we were not.

As I breathe a sigh of relief a number of the team appear, and we quickly unload the boxes and ever-more boxes of biscuits onto the pavement. About 30 minutes later the main foyer is stacked with boxes like a delivery of parcels for freight.

What on earth are we going to do with all these biscuits! We can't sell this much at the cake and candy stalls. At that moment, a lightbulb went off in my head "how not to make a drama out of a crisis."

Every floor has catering, we will sell them to each business (still cheaper than their current suppliers), and we can donate the money to the charities.

My fun day turned into a sales-negotiation frenzy. Delighted we managed to pull this one off.

This was close, note to self "You didn't take the time to understand or explore what 'ALL things biscuit' really meant." Thank God, I was around and in my trainers.

So how did I even become Top Cat you are probably wondering and what's the difference between Top Cat and Boss Cat?

Some folks are naturally good or experienced in a particular area.

In my world, this was employee relations, TUPE, Transfer of Undertakings (Protection of Employment) Regulations 2006, Trade Unions and of course ACAS, Advisory, Conciliation and Arbitration Service. This meant that the difficult stuff tended to come my way.

On a number of occasions comments were made like "TC can you help, this is a minefield." "Hey Top Cat bet you can fix this issue." These became daily comments to the point that although my initials were TC, Top Cat was taking on a whole identity of its own.

One day I overhead a colleague say to another "Listen that's no kitten, you need Top Cat, leader of the pack to solve that mess"

The kitten had clearly turned into a cat and my claws were sharpened. So Top Cat stuck and let's be honest, I'd been called worse, even if my mantra was "Always wear your pants outside your trousers like Superwoman" which would have never accommodated my tail.

But my pearls of wisdom continued and being a HR Professional can bring a lot of pain before the joy! A bit like childbirth but it's all worth it in the end even if motherhood can be a tad overrated at times.

So now Boss Cat had simply arrived in the Tom Cat environment to undertake the male domination that existed in so many working environments.

The higher up the ladder you progress, more and more often you are the only female. Unbelievably, male groups somehow find a way to separate you from their pack in name terms, or what they believe 'terms of endearment'

This time, no Boss or Top just "Treacle."

To this day I think it was as it began with a "T" and stuck well to my personality. Don't be fooled by this being protective or precious.

On one occasion a clear instruction was given to 8 senior directors. "No one moves until she finishes speaking and draws breath. Do you get me. We need this people mess fixed."

That was a real boss move on his part. He made it clear that the most important person to fix this problem was about to speak and the crew were going to listen. A slight change in approach but the "the most powerful and the most important" was a play on words which elevated me tenfold.

And if you are wondering, this chap was a first-class top act that we need more of at the Senior Directorship levels.

Sometimes it's like finding the impossible solution, but we get there.

In summary Top Cat flourished at being the best at everything HR related whilst Boss Cat managed everything and everyone in the vicinity.

CHAPTER 7: Top Cat to Boss Cat

CHAPTER 8
POWER
STILETTOS AND FLIPFLOPS

"

Give a girl the
right shoes
and she can
conquer the
world.

- Marilyn Monroe

"

Footwear in HR has its place.

You can be standing in the largest Boardroom with killer heels feeling like a 'lamb to the slaughter,' but if you always think about putting your best foot forward, you will not go far, wrong.

You see recruitment can be like shoe sales.

I should know as I have accomplished both. A summer job selling shoes, handbags and all the extra sprays, shines, and protectors that you can possibly imagine. It is called selling fancies, remember Sales pay for everything. Fancy That! Recruitment is not that different when we present the right human beings.

A job search will generate good candidates. However, it will also drive a strong finder's fee, and the more placements, the more fees.

Stands to reason especially in good shoes: One could say if the shoe fits wear it!

However, one thing that HR is very good at is the 'Work Hard, Play Hard Mentality'. This is not to be confused with working harder not smarter. Here the shoe is required to be on the other foot and fit like Cinderella's.

I remain forever focused on the fact that "Lets employ the best people and get out of their way." However, this cannot be said for some trainees or graduates ...

As an HR Graduate back in the good old days, the rota provided for a wide range of experiences in many parts of a business, not just HR.

Nowadays, we sometimes have smart-assed graduates. Before we even have a chance to help encourage a vision for their development, they are already blind-sided by what they think HR is. They are too resolute about what they are not going to do, rather than embracing the HR culture and processes.

Let's always remember, folks 'Don't know what they don't know'. Often the University of Life experience is lacking at all ages and all stages of their so far brief career.

I remember I was asked to take a recently appointed graduate to a meeting with me, as an observer. As all great professionals, we plan and prepare, and this meeting was no different. We took some time in the morning to go over the meeting agenda and what may be discussed.

To say the chap was disinterested, was an understatement. He was slouched in the chair and may as well have been wearing summer short and flip flops, he was that uninterested. He took the stance that having covered finance in his third-year studies, final salary pensions, and so to actuaries, were a dying breed and quite frankly "a walk in the park".

My initial thoughts were to postpone his attendance. However, everyone needs to learn sometime.

On arrival at the meeting, he was not the only graduate. A beautiful young girl who probably should have been a model, walked into the meeting with her chaperone. She was without a doubt, absolutely dressed to impress, and with the highest stilettos I have ever seen! I continued to observe and think, "does she have different foot arches from every other human on the planet? And do these kids actually eat, like ever eat?"

She sat down and my graduate observer was clearly now in "Let's impress mode."   To my dismay he immediately went into free fall. As opposed to observing, verbal diarrhoea ensued, but not in a professional way.

His catty young 'Chappy' laughs and giggles were clearly annoying the Chair! Immediately the Chair blurted out "Tracey a word!". Shocked, I quickly slipped my toes back into my stiletto's, stood up, and strutted behind him into the corridor.

His face was bright red, and his eyes were black and menacing.

"Let me be clear, we don't have time for this. Get your mutt back on his leash now before I remove the two of you."

In that moment, my advice is to stand back, stand tall and clearly speak eloquently. That is exactly what TC did.

 "I hear your message, and feel your pain. However, he's not my graduate, but I shall deal with this."

He moved like a tank in action, and trundled towards the unisex toilet. I spun 180 degrees like a ballerina on pointe and opened the door.

Smiling in friendly overtones, "Rupert I would like a word". He stands up, buttons his jacket and swaggers towards me.

As we are outside the meeting room, I lower the tone of my voice, "Do you understand observation?"

His non-verbal response was a smarmy grin, like a Cheshire Cat.

 "Well, it's not obvious in my observations that your behaviour is appropriate for this meeting. Rupert, as an observer you either go back in there and be quiet, or you go home."

The go-home part landed the deal. He looked at me like a little boy lost, and said, "Absolutely.   I just got a bit carried away with Emily. You know she has a zillion followers on Instagram!

For the Love of God, I wondered if HR Shared Services thoroughly checked all social media platforms? Note to self: check the process.

Then, I realise Rupert is still talking and drooling over Emily. "OMG you should see her beach range!"

As I raise my eyebrow, tilt my head like a meerkat, almost inaudible say "Enough. Now, let's get back into that room, Flipflop."

The next 45 minutes felt like 2 hours. It was clearly another time in my life that I would never get back. Just before the very end of the tortuous meeting, both graduates were asked if they had any feedback. The adorable Emily eloquently explains that she understood more clearly now about the role of the pension actuary. Flipflop, pushed his chair back folded his legs and placed his clasped hands, on his knee as if he were a TV interviewer, and deliberated, "Absolutely, same as Emily, it has been a pleasure."

Whit! Well at least he only said nine words, his nine lives were nearly over and Top Cat was not going to be taking Flipflop anywhere again soon. What is it they say, "never work with children or animals!"

On reflection, it was clear that Flipflop, who had the gift of the gab, was the polar opposite of his competitive counterpart whom I interviewed the day before. The poor boy Roy, despite being a first-class honours engineering graduate, only managed a few words, went a peculiar colour, much more than a whiter shade of pale, stood up, picked up the interview room bin and threw up.

Poor Roy, the boy who barfed in the bin, will never get over the experience and neither will I. His suit and the carpet tiles which were so pebble dashed they all died an instant death. Thankfully Roy got to interview on another day. This time he had been a good boy the night before, refrained from fraternising with Flipflop, knew to keep away from the dizzy heights of the windows on the 17th Floor and landed his dream job.

Such experiences lead HR into new projects such as, Drugs & Alcohol testing in the late 90's. This was a new training project for HR. In the beginning it became an extension of the HR role. However, this needed to quickly involve and move to management.

In the past, a blind eye was often turned. However, with sporting events and seasonal occasions such as Festive party, the Monday absence – Friday awol behaviour became out of control. As Health & Safety evolved, Drugs & Alcohol Testing became the norm. Recruitment requirements and random testing became the norm to tackle the matter in hand.

Even today, HR are more about pass the Champagne, please!

However, the twice-daily tea trolley, with hot rolls in the morning and scones in the afternoon, which were to die for, was the highlight of the day. Despite this, Jessie the tea-trolly lady was never without her wee sherry! The "drinks" trolly took on an entirely different new meaning during the festive period. Back then, Personnel, alias HR, would prepare the "drinks" trolley. A senior manager, always a male and the only time ever to be seen pushing a trolley, would glide round the building and offer staff festive refreshments which were clearly not tea and biscuits. The reason it was a male was simply, when it was everyday stuff, like common or garden tea Jessie would suffice. However, when it was the good stuff i.e. booze, a senior manager was bestowed that honour.

On one occasion when the bacon rolls were in short supply, it instigated a ballot for a walk out. However, that was not as bad as when the local farmers ran out of turkeys. It was that serious that it was necessary to go out and buy vouchers for replacement turkeys to avert full strike action. That's why turkeys don't vote for Christmas.

Back on the Festive spirit, employed drivers were also in on the case. In order to avoid the risk of being over-the-limit on the morning after, the said drivers would administer co-codamol to themselves to prevent them from driving under the influence and not positive in the testing criteria. This circumvention of the policy was soon spotted and more attention to prescription meds and drivers' behaviour patterns were dealt with.

The more employees travelled the globe, the more drug issues HR

had to deal with. This was now way beyond over-the-counter or prescribed medication. The issue flip flopped time and time again. Opiates, hallucinogens and benzodiazepines should be avoided. Some drugs, which are legal abroad, can take up to Ten to Twelve weeks to pass through a human being's system. This is an absolute nightmare when you are involved in random drugs testing, which is still more commonly used than we think today. So, the next time, someone offers you a 'cookie' or a 'cake' in a European Bar, read the menu, as it will definitely not have a label!

In those days, we were cutting our teeth on the 'D & A' Testing. Not only did we not have much of a clue about drug potency, we were still working our way through the alcoholic content of a bottle of beer and a boozy breezier.

So, it's still more champagne please!

Today, regardless of what industry you are involved in, there is a definitive Drugs & Alcohol Policy, consistent in the wider community. It is no longer feasible to simply turn up 'one over the eight'. No Human Being is above and beyond flip flopping on the issues of drugs and alcohol. There is no place for delusion, or the opportunity to authorise your unauthorised abuse of power.

Despite whether we are strutting our stuff in the Boardroom in stilettos, or sitting in our pyjama bottoms wearing funky slippers on Zoom, understanding that being 'in a place of power' and having confidence, is the key to success. Even 'M' proclaimed that he could do more sitting in his pyjamas before he finished his first cup of 'Earl Grey, than Bond could do in the field.

The outcome of any power struggle today is to create a work-life balance. Hybrid working means that working from home is possible as well as working in the office.

The demarcation lines have become blurred of when work and homelife start and stop. An easy way to think about this is footwear.

Flipflops at the ready. It is no longer a workday "please remove sand before proceeding" or let's just party. Whether expensive Havana's or simply cheap ones, they have taken on a new lease on life. They are still not suitable as safety footwear for work, or for barbeques as highlighted in the health-and-safety adverts of the past. Such scenes of the worker halfway up a ladder, wearing a hardhat and no footwear, bare feet at the ready are passe. Here their flip flops might even have helped!. However, there was never a complaint made, and the workers were as happy as Larry.

Today, the 'Constant Complainers' that do complain all day about everything and anything, will finally find themselves confronted by HR. Without doubt, the HR Troops are ready for them, just like human remains. It's a pity they didn't keep the sand in the flip flops, that would turn into pearls of wisdom.

These 'Constant Complainers' are the most irritating of all. They can be the gals who rock back and forward in the HR hotseat chair across the desk from the HR Manager being on output only whilst talking and complaining at the same time. Then there are the guys who perform the manoeuvre, 'moving flamingo'. Only this time, here they are placing the shoes on their knees as if they are performing an Irish jig whilst sitting down. As they talk and complain about practically everything, they frantically untie and tie their shoelaces, one shoe, then repeat on the other side. This strange manoeuvre always makes me surprised that they could tie their shoelaces in the first place.

In Summary, whether you're wearing Christian Louboutin's, Havana's, Balenciaga, Dior Loafers or Russell & Bromley and that's just the gents! Remember to shake off those pins and needles and strut your Stuff, whilst sipping Dolce & Gabbana red wine is a must unless your name is Rupert of course!

P.S. Apologies no advertising rights and revenue to be achieved.

"

Don't be a hard rock when you really are a gem!

- By Lauryn Hill

CHAPTER 9
THE HARD ROCK OF HR

So, the Hard Rock of HR!

Let me tell you, this is a tough gig. When drama occurs in business and folks' jobs are on the line, the one team who are working day and night is HR. Whether you receive an email, call, or invite to speak with HR during this celestial time. panic reigns.

The employees will be thinking about one thing, not me. The battle cry is "it's not me." But the thing is, a role is made redundant not a person. Other War cries are 'I'm not taking any bloody package. I know too much and all the skeletons in the closet.'

During significant change, I've been called the 'Angel of Death.' Another one was "Look,here is the 'Grim Reaper' coming again." However, someone needs to manage redundancies and trust me it is better to have an expert in your midst rather than an amateur. So, wipe your Flip Flops, move on and stop complaining.

Talking about the 'Constant Complainers' when they aren't even affected by redundancy, their complaints range from the preposterous to nonsense. Let's think now:

I need a new chair	I hate my new laptop	I don't like sitting in an office
I don't like hot desking	It's too hot	It's too cold
The windows need cleaning	The desk wobbles	The aircon is too loud

That clock's slow

We should have our own bins; it takes ages to recycle

Why are drinks on a Friday after work and not in the afternoon

Really! Notice this is mostly about the "I's" and they are not even on notice.

This behaviour is not restricted to the lower ranks, it pervades the senior ranks as well. Selfishness is a disregard of others and again knows no bounds. It is all about being concerned only with oneself. This is a challenge for HR. Leadership traits and behaviours of a selfish leader is about those who lead with more emphasis on themselves. This can undoubtedly lead to toxic settings that goes far beyond the work environment.

I attended a senior leadership workshop on 'Insights', the 360-colour part of the personal insight's leadership program and key to working collaboratively:

Fiery Red Energy = competitive, demanding, determined, strong-willed and purposeful

Cool Blue Energy = cautious, precise, deliberate, questioning, and formal

Sunshine Yellow Energy = sociable, dynamic, demonstrative, enthusiastic and persuasive

Earth Green Energy = caring, encouraging, sharing, patient and relaxed

My leadership style would naturally say 'Red/Yellow, Fiery and Sunshine'. In fact, that's exactly what the results of the program were. The instruction on the day was to collect a hat that reflected your leadership style. Arriving at the red-hat station, I was confronted by another female director advising, "she was the only red in the room." It is rather difficult to watch a female director try to take command of a room of senior leaders in hats, shouting "I'm the leader". It is not necessary to be the Top Cat at all times. Just know who respects and follows you.

Another area that is tough to manage in HR is 'Pillow Talk'. Employees have affairs, relationships, marriages, and even divorces. Work social events have an amazing impact on normally, well-behaved human beings. The most peculiar partner matches emerge, and the gossip invariably becomes the reality. Confidentiality is always a challenge as people love to be the first to tell.

Maybe you work in Finance and a budget cut is looming, this is on a need-to-know basis and only HR and Finance know this information. However, your bed fellow works in another department and all of a sudden the rumours spill in Marketing. This is exactly where your partner works. HR now know exactly where the leak came from. The moral of the story is, if you are bound by confidentiality honour it, because you can only break trust once.

I turned up at the Christmas Night out for the pre-dinner drinks. Staff were already dancing around chairs in the middle of the dance floor, partially dressed and looking as if they were brawling in a brothel scene in a movie. Super pretty, amazing dancers with UV illuminated costumes were the act of the night. People should be able to go to their work, regardless of what their vocation is, without the need for a sign saying, "Don't touch the Act". Needless to say, the cabaret was halted. The Christmas night disseminated into an evening of the slosh and the time warp all at the same time. The message for the next social was don't touch the entertainers. For the managers HR always advise, its best not to sleep with the staff.

To lighten the mood, HR does not always have to be about this heavy-handed reality of Hard Rock HR. And remember you can play on the swings as well as the roundabout. Every dog has its day, don't let people get under your skin. The rotten apples will emerge and the good folks are like cream that rise to the top.

When we talk about the 5 "S", we talk about a method of organising a workspace.

The amazing thing about Japanese methodology, is that it uses the 5 "S". And at this moment, not a stiletto in sight. And these are:

Sorting: Eliminate all unnecessary tools part and instructions

Straightening/Setting Order: arrange work areas in frequently used ways to eliminate time wasting

Sweeping or Shine: Clean, tidy, and organised

Standardising: If employees do the same job work areas are identical

Sustaining: Maintain the same configuration over time

Technically these 5 'S' are not the sexy, shiny stuff, but how to organise a workstation for uniformity.   However, working on these as the basic strategy and allowing an individual to personalise their workstation is just one way of bringing out the best in people.

If we focus on having the right people, then rudiments of HR: Recruitment, Selection, Performance Management, Learning, & Development and Succession Planning simply flourish.

One of the less desirable hard knocks for HR experts is when people don't know what they don't know.

Sometimes you will find diamonds in the mud, they are just rough around the edges and need your expert help and advice.

If anything, Shine bright like a Diamond!

"

I knew that 2 years of Latin study would come in useful one day, even if it is not a widely spoken language, seize the day!

- By Tracey Chrystal, HR Expert

"

CHAPTER 10

TIME

TIME, IS A RARE COMMODITY YOU CANNOT BUY

> **" Carpe Diem, one should enjoy life while one can!**
>
> – By Roman Poet, Horace **"**

Time waits for no one. Therefore, we must use our time wisely. Laughter is timeless, imagination has no age and dreams are forever so why is time like roulette? One minute you're graduating the next minute you are addressing graduates as they embark on their HR journey.

I remember attending a work social event and a group of graduates were partying and banging their arms on the tables to "I'd like to move it, move it, I'd like to move it, move it" from the movie, Madagascar. By the end of the night, they had no concept of time, as they had no hands on their watches, let alone a glass face. Not sure how an iPhone watch compares these days however back then it seemed as if time was slower and in that moment they had all the time in the world.

Hour glasses are pretty to watch as the sand quickly falls, however only if you are holding on for a team or zoom call to start, or otherwise, you are just wasting your time unless you need this for boiling an egg or something!

I attended a time management course which advised keep a timer near your phone or pc and only allow for 15 minutes for unplanned calls. I get the essence of this, however if someone is calling about a new piece of work and using your services you are hardly going to cut them off at 15 minutes if 18 minutes is required.

So how can we best manage and preserve our time? Lets consider the folks that simply drain your time. Why listen to someone that takes 30 minutes to say something that can be said in 5? Watch out for the busy fools, and folks who attend lots of events, want to network excessively however, never get any work done. Often you give them more help and advice, that you don't charge for and more time you will never get back.

I have coached many people over the past few years unable to manage their time. Often they are over worked, under resourced, time shy, no boundaries for work life balance as working from home has no end point whilst having to deal with a number of time wasters who drain their very soul.

My main concern is there is a fine balance between being unable to manage time, being and feeling overwhelmed and burn out. The main challenge is often by the time this is recognised, it is too late. The person has become completely exhausted through overwork and this presents itself as a physical ailment where they have passed slow down and need to stop. The latter which is clearly not their intention.

One minute you are on your career path, the next you are looking back over the years and wondering where the time has gone. Someone said to me recently "Yip, one minute you're young hip and carefree, the next minute you're taking pictures of flowers in the garden." Glad I currently have a balcony and not a garden then!

So, how do we combat this – final refresher learning:

✓　　　Knowing when to take a break

✓　　　Try not to lose sight of who you are

✓　　　Go for that 30-minute walk, get some fresh air

✓　　　Clear your head

✓　　　Recognise when you need head space

✓　　　Sharpen up your delegation skills

✓　　　Think about outcomes and not actions

✓　　　Avoid the time wasters and the busy fools

✓　　　Take an online time management refresher course

✓　　　Learn how to say "no"

We can't buy time, it's a rare commodity, we simply need to manage it better.

In an instant world we need to stop sweating the small stuff and instil this approach with our clients. Lets not put off till tomorrow what we can do today. Why?

Because tomorrow may be too late. Think about quick, short meetings rather than 2 hours here and 4 hours there, unless they are absolutely necessary. Why travel an hour each way when you can meet online, even every second catch up.

Eliminate blockers, identify what is getting in the way. What could you stop doing today verses what you must do.

Data from the National Centre for Health US, advises that the average person in a lifetime does the following:

Activity	Hours
Sleeps	229,961
Watches TV	80,486
Drives	37,935
Eats	32,098
Surf the Internet	28,300
Works	**90,360**

That's a lot of **working hours!.**

Life is simply too short, and this ain't a dress rehearsal.

Thank you for joining me on this honesty trip of HR, where you simply couldn't make this stuff up!

No one ever said on their death bed "I should have worked longer hours" therefore, don't let Human Resources become Human Remains!

Kick back and live a lot!

And finally on a visual note please view the Chrystal HR & Coaching Videos on www.chrystalhr.com where you will find more interesting facts about HR, coaching and consultancy. Highlighting the key reasons for working with Chrystal HR from Peace of mind through consistently advising Everything Everyday whilst getting it right.

WAYS TO CONNECT WITH TRACEY

https://www.linkedin.com/in/tracey-chrystal-96291232

tchrystal@chrystalhr.com

https://www.chrystahr.com

TESTIMONALS

Chrystal HR have supported our business for the past 4 years through some very challenging times post Covid. During this period the Group have grown from 25 to 48 staff, Chrystal HR's support has been invaluable in helping us through the growth. Tracey Chrystal's response has always been timely, knowledgeable, flexible, and exceptionally good.

Engineering/Manufacturing Firm, Erskine

Chrystal Training were excellent at delivering online training on "Understanding our legal responsibilities when employing people," I selected eight of my managers to attend and they found the course in valuable and delivered in a clear and easy to understand way, Highly Recommended.

Manufacturing Firm, Dumfries

High performing teams is a key ethos for our business. Working with Chrystal Training was outstanding, they delivered a 2-day workshop covering our full team and really helped us understand each other and how we interacted. Guidance, advice, and behaviours for a high performing team culture was profound as was exploring our team dynamics and those with our clients.

Tax Specialists, Edinburgh

Not everyone wants to undergo significant change but if they do, we can thoroughly recommend Chrystal HR & Training, their approach to change management and leading successful change was empowering and really helped us upskill in this area which helped us save time and act with pace. Strongly Recommended.

Logistics Firm, Glasgow

Tracey's experience extends to recruitment, training, employee relations, coaching, HR Health Checks, employment contracts, policy and procedures refresh, restructure, business change, mediation and pretty much all aspects of employing an individual from onboarding to redundancy or retirement for a wide variety of clients.

Tracey is a strong, clear communicator, who is always professional and discreet. We are all excited to be working with her and know she will add great value to our clients.

HR Consultancy Firm, Glasgow

ACKNOWLEDGEMENTS

I would like to say a heartfelt thank you to my amazing daughter Courtney, who took the time and patience to contribute some drawings in the book.

To the talented Fiona Taylor and The Business Book Blueprint, who ensures that your creative expression is fully explored.

Thank you to all my colleagues, especially those who have made HR enjoyable. I am sure you may recognise some of the characters in the book.

Keep that grey matter ticking, try a quick word search!

Word Search

P	B	A	M	C	O	A	C	H	I	N	G	G	E
S	M	E	E	T	I	N	G	N	Z	E	W	T	V
Y	I	L	B	O	A	R	D	E	X	E	C	R	E
C	P	B	E	A	T	E	A	C	H	E	R	A	N
H	D	R	C	A	C	Z	B	L	G	E	F	I	T
O	F	S	O	B	D	A	M	Z	A	B	X	N	P
L	B	K	P	J	T	E	S	A	Z	I	N	I	L
O	S	F	R	A	E	R	R	U	N	N	L	N	A
G	H	J	Q	K	R	C	I	S	C	A	X	G	N
I	I	A	M	L	K	K	T	B	H	C	G	M	N
S	N	S	C	J	Z	O	L	S	U	I	E	E	E
T	E	A	M	L	E	A	D	E	R	N	P	S	R
D	S	G	R	I	E	V	A	N	C	E	A	V	S
D	I	S	C	I	P	L	I	N	E	N	I	L	T

BOARDEXEC
TRIBUNAL
TEAMLEADER
SUCCESS
PSYCHOLOGIST
MEETING
ACAS
COACHING
EVENTPLANNER
SPARKLE
DISCIPLINE
TRAINING
TEACHER
SHINE
GRIEVANCE

Word Search Answers

P	B	A	M	C	O	A	C	H	I	N	G	G	E
S	M	E	E	T	I	N	G	N	Z	E	W	T	V
Y	I	L	B	O	A	R	D	E	X	E	C	R	E
C	P	B	E	A	T	E	A	C	H	E	R	A	N
H	D	R	C	A	C	Z	B	L	G	E	F	I	T
O	F	S	O	B	D	A	M	Z	A	B	X	N	P
L	B	K	P	J	T	E	S	A	Z	I	N	I	L
O	S	F	R	A	E	R	R	U	N	N	L	N	A
G	H	J	Q	K	R	C	I	S	C	A	X	G	N
I	I	A	M	L	K	K	T	B	H	C	G	M	N
S	N	S	C	J	Z	O	L	S	U	I	E	E	E
T	E	A	M	L	E	A	D	E	R	N	P	S	R
D	S	G	R	I	E	V	A	N	C	E	A	V	S
D	I	S	C	I	P	L	I	N	E	N	I	L	T

BOARDEXEC
TRIBUNAL
TEAMLEADER
SUCCESS
PSYCHOLOGIST
MEETING
ACAS
COACHING
EVENTPLANNER
SPARKLE
DISCIPLINE
TRAINING
TEACHER
SHINE
GRIEVANCE

HUMAN RESOURCES
NOT HUMAN REMAINS

This book is for you, to give you a glance into the realms of HR along with the people nuances. It is a snapshot and brief encounter of HR gained through knowledge and experience over the years. It provides a sharing of HR knowledge through fun stories and lessons learned. Where emotional feelings are almost like the fall out of a car crash, when things go wrong and scary and we need to minimise the blow. Not like a car crash, the end result is for HR to be unscathed and unscared by Human Remains. The purpose of the book is to influence the HR Industry and HR Community that it is all right to talk about the taboo subjects.

My gift to you is to maintain professional integrity at all times and enjoy the stories as they are meant to be fun. HR is really the School of HR, and all that it does.

ABOUT THE AUTHOR

Tracey Chrystal is a professional business owner and director with over 30 years' experience. She is a qualified CIPD Level 7 Chartered Fellow, ILM7 Executive Coach (MInstLM) and Board Director. As a member of the Institute of Directors, Tracey has a strategy focus and insures business strategy is aligned to the business requirements. She works proactively and collaboratively with senior leaders to ensure optimum business delivery.

Tracey established an HR Consultancy & Coaching business on the back of a dynamic professional career. An expert in the field of Human Resources and seen as a thought and influencing leader. Working with some of the largest companies on the globe, my international assignments have taken me to India, USA, Europe and widely across the UK. With extensive HR Experience of over 30 years plus, there have been highs and lows on my journey however, my legacy will be that I continue to grow with integrity and stay true to my authentic self.